The Truth About Troth

The Teutonic tradition is as rich and varied as the Hermetic or Kabbalistic systems—in fact, this largely ignored and often misunderstood system of magickal practice has actually been a major influence on the Western Occult tradition.

Teutonic magick and spirituality offer seekers a great wealth of lore and beliefs, all of which are illuminated in *The Truth About Teutonic Magick*:

- the concept of *troth*, the faith of the Teutons, as embodied in the Icelandic sagas and Northern folklore
- a rich pantheon of divine magickal archetypes
- an ancient runic language, which encodes cosmic mysteries
- the eight sacred festivals and how they're celebrated
- a Teutonic form of shamanism involving altered states of consciousness and travel to the nine magickal realms

The Teutonic tradition is attracting increasing interest among students of High Magick. This book offers a quick, thorough understanding of the principles underlying this timeless magickal system for anyone who's curious

About the Author

Edred Thorsson is well known as the author of *Futhark: A Handbook of Rune Magic, Runelore: A Handbook of Esoteric Runology, At the Well of Wyrd: A Handbook of Runic Divination, Rune Might* and *A Book of Troth*. Since 1972, he has been dedicated to the esoteric and exoteric study of the Indo-European, Celtic and Teutonic traditions. He studied Old Irish, Middle Welsh and Indo-European religion and culture at major universities in Germany and in the United States.

To Write to the Author

If you wish to contact the author or would like more information about this book, please write to the author in care of Llewellyn Worldwide and we will forward your request. Both the author and publisher appreciate hearing from you and learning of your enjoyment of this book and how it has helped you. Llewellyn Worldwide cannot guarantee that every letter written to the author can be answered, but all will be forwarded. Please write to:

Edred Thorsson
c/o Llewellyn Worldwide
P.O. Box 64383-779, St. Paul, MN 55164-0383, U.S.A.

Please enclose a self-addressed, stamped envelope for reply, or
$1.00 to cover costs.
If outside U.S.A., enclose International postal reply coupon.

Free Catalog From Llewellyn

For more than 90 years Llewellyn has brought its readers knowledge in the fields of metaphysics and human potential. Learn about the newest books in spiritual guidance, natural healing, astrology, occult philosophy, and more. Enjoy book reviews, new age articles, a calender of events, plus current products and services. To get your free copy of *Llewellyn's New Worlds of Mind and Spirit*, send your name and address to:

Llewellyn's New Worlds of Mind and Spirit
P.O. Box 64383-779, St. Paul, MN 55164-0383, U.S.A.

A LLEWELLYN'S VANGUARD SERIES

The Truth About

TEUTONIC MAGICK

by Edred Thorsson

Author of
Book of Ogham, Book of Troth, Nine Doors of Midgard, Northern Magic, Rune Might

1994
Llewellyn Publications
St. Paul, MN 55164-0383, U.S.A.

FIRST EDITION, 1989
SECOND EDITION
First Printing, 1994

International Standard Book Number:
0-87542-799-0

LLEWELLYN PUBLICATIONS
A Division of Llewellyn Worldwide, Ltd.
P.O. Box 64383, St. Paul, MN 55164-0383

Llewellyn Publications is the oldest publisher of New Age Sciences in the Western Hemisphere. This book is one of a series of introductory explorations of each one of the many fascinating dimensions of New Age Science— each important to a new understanding of Body and Soul, Mind and Spirit, of Nature and humanity's place in the world, and the vast unexplored regions of Microcosm and Macrocosm.

Please write for a full list of publications.

INTRODUCTION

On a lonely windswept hill under the boughs of a gnarled oak, a man in a blue cloak carves elder runes in a stave of yew wood. He calls out the names of the runes in the tongue used by his ancestors 2,000 years ago—forging a direct link between himself and the holy power of the runes and between his time and place and that of his ancestors.

Several dozen folks gather themselves before an altar of stone glinting with the rays of the midsummer's sun and sing out the songs of celebration, giving holy gifts to their elder gods for everlasting peace and prosperity. In this time and in this place they have become whole with the spirit of their ancestral troth, or faith.

High atop a wooden platform a woman sits in trance, her long blue cape flowing around her. The low chants of her helpers take her down into a world she knows well, and from which she will bring wisdom and lore about times gone by and of times yet to be.

All of these folks are practicing forms of what can be called Teutonic magick. Teutonic magick is essentially the whole spectrum of magickal and spiritual disciplines and traditions practiced by the Teutons over the expanse of time, beginning when this eldritch folk emerged from the mists until the present day.

It is practically impossible to present the whole truth of a religious tradition or a system of magick practiced by an entire group of people over hundreds of years. There are, however, great truths and deep secrets about how the Teutonic folk practiced their troth and magick in days of yore and how they practice them now that will be of interest to all who read this little book.

Here we will explore not one but several great traditions of Teutonic magick. We will look at the essence of rune magick and of seidhr—the two main practices of the timeless and pure forms of Teutonic magickal practice. We will examine the traditions of the great troth of the Teutons, or their religious faith as it is practiced today. Furthermore, we will take a look at the magickal teachings that have been influenced, shaped, or reformed by the Teutonic mind and that have subsequently become the occult standards of the Western Tradition.

WHO ARE THE TEUTONS?

The Teutons are known from ancient times as a group of people who originally spoke the Germanic dialect group of languages. Some prefer to use the term "Teutonic" to avoid the confusion between the words "Germanic" and "German." But in reality the terms "Teutonic" and "Germanic" are synonymous. Directly descended from this ancient Teutonic stock are the English, German, Dutch, Icelandic, Danish, Norwegian, and Swedish peoples. What is more, they left their indelible mark on the cultures of the French, Spanish, and Italian nations, as they founded the first true states in those lands after the fall of the Roman Empire. These people not only had a tradition of religion and mythology unique to themselves (although closely related to their other Indo-European brethren the Celts, Slavs, Romans, Greeks,

Persians, and Indians) but they also had a unique magickal system that has come down to us for the most part in the form of rune magick.

The magickal and religious teachings of these people are most clearly laid out in the ancient texts known as the Eddas, of which there is a younger, or prose, version, and an elder, or poetic, version. In these works are encoded the mysteries of the Teutonic peoples. These can be understood on many levels.

In the elder days there were many more sources of the tradition, but the Christian missionaries destroyed many of them. The chief target of their ire seems to have been the teachings and traditions surrounding the goddess Freya, whose poetry and songs (many of them eroto-magickal) were singled out for utter obliteration.

The traditions that survived the best were those connected to the god Woden, whose loyalists were to be found in the Teutonic royal houses—somewhat insulated from the influences of the new religion. This circumstance is somewhat responsible for the misguided assumption that the Teutonic tradition is a male-dominated one. This is not especially true; it is just a matter of what has been able to survived in the written tradition. Now is the time to revive fully the elder ways of the goddess Freya.

In modern times the Teutonic stream of magick has been largely ignored during the great magickal revival in the Western world. There were revivals of the Germanic tradition in the 1500s and 1600s in Sweden, and in the late 1800s and early 1900s in Germany, but only in the past 20 years or so have there been any worldwide attempts at the revival of the ancient ways of the Teutons. At present, there are many groups in the United States and Europe engaged in the work of reviving the elder traditions of the Teutonic folk.

The practice of the Teutonic forms of magick is the birthright of most readers of this book by virtue of the fact that you have been born into the life-stream of an English-speaking (Teutonic) nation. This is your most natural, organic tradition to deal with magically. You already "speak its language" in the most literal sense.

The Teutonic tradition of magick has long suffered from two kinds of problems. First, there has been a vast ignorance concerning its existence and its deep roots in the "folk-soul." The native organic traditions of the Europeans—be they Celtic or Teutonic—were submerged under the false cultural prestige of the Greco-Roman and Judeo-Christian worlds. This burden was only thrown off with the help of the scholarship and magickal work of the past 200 years. This research showed what vast, natural, authentic magickal and religious traditions are to be found in our own cultures. The second problem has been the misguided use of these traditions. In this century we have seen how Teutonic symbolism has been used not to liberate but to enslave and destroy. This does not necessarily have anything to do with the true practice of Teutonic magick, but it does show the incredible storehouse of power available in its symbolism.

THE TEUTONIC MAGICIAN

As there are several distinct kinds of Teutonic magick, so too are there several dis-

tinct kinds of Teutonic magicians. The first
kind is not really a magician in the strictest
sense, but rather a priest or priestess. This
is the Elder of the Troth, sometimes also
known by the Old Norse terms godhi
("goh-thee") or gydhja ("gith-ya") for the
male and female respectively. The other
two kinds of magicians in the narrower
sense—those who seek not only to main-
tain or restore the sacred order of the universe but also to make changes in it in
accordance with their own wills—are the
practitioners of galster and seidhr ("say-
ther"). Both may be known by the general
Old Norse term vitki, meaning "wise one."

Whether for religious or magickal
purposes, the practitioner of true Teutonic
magick must undergo a period of preparation before the right pathways can be fol-
lowed. This preparation comes in two
forms. First the would-be vitki must steep
him/herself in the lore of the Teutons. The
mythology, legends and lore—the cos-
mologies and theologies—should be
learned so that thinking in such terms
becomes virtually natural. For those interested in becoming runemasters, the runic

tradition must also be learned in a similar way. This provides a traditional "inner landscape" for further work that is authentic and accurate, so that work done within it cannot lead you astray but instead will further insight. The second part of a would-be vitki's preparation can be undertaken simultaneously with the first. This is basic training in concentration and visualization. This latter element is common to success in any form of magick. However, one of the main elements of current Teutonic magick is the will to link the self with the higher principles of the folk-soul. For this purpose to be fulfilled, the first element is absolutely essential.

The Teutonic magician, or vitki, is a very independent sort. In ancient times as well as today, many prefer to work alone or in very small groups, loosely affiliated within a guild. (This is not true of the religious tradition which seeks to involve the whole community.) The independence of the Teutonic magician goes beyond the social aspect and is also exemplified in his or her magickal character. The vitki—and especially the runemaster—does not normally

seek the magickal aid of magickal forces outside himself, but rather seeks to influence the
course of events directly. The standard of the
medieval magician evoking and coercing
angels or demons to do his bidding by the
power of supposedly higher forces outside
himself are almost totally foreign to the Teutonic mode of magickal working.

THE TEUTONIC MAGICKAL WORLD

In the Teutonic view of the world and of
humanity, there have always been many
dimensions or worlds. In the larger world,
or macrocosm, this is illustrated in the lore
concerning the World-Tree, Yggdrasill.
This "tree" is said to consist of nine realms
or worlds, the symbolic arrangement of
which can be seen in Figure 1. The actual
arrangement of the worlds could not be
effected in two or three dimensions, as it is
always clear in every account that the tree
is really a symbol of a multidimensional
construct of some kind.

Asgard is the kingdom of the Æsir,
and of those Vanir who have come to live
among the Æsir. Hel is the realm of the

dead and of the forces of universal dissolution. Lightelf-Home is the kingdom of the elves (demigods and divinized ancestral spirits). This is the dimension of the structures of the intellect. Opposite this is Swartelf-Home. "Swartelf" is another name for dwarf. The dwarves, like the Lightelves, are essentially ancestral spirits or demigods (or perhaps demons?). The dwarves are, however, not of an intellectual nature but rather embody the structuralizing and formative forces in the world. Wane-Home is the realm of the Wanes, or Vanir, which are further described below. Opposite this is Ettin-Home, which is the realm of primeval forces of blind, non-conscious chaos and/or order. An "ettin" is a non-conscious construct. The realms of Muspell-Home and Nifel-Home are the realms of cosmic fire and ice respectively. It is from these two extremes of cosmic activity that the universe comes into being. Between and among all of these opposing forces is the realm of all potential, the blessed land of Midgard—the enclosure in the midst of all. In it lives humankind, the only other entity in the cosmos that shares the gift of consciousness with the gods and goddesses.

THE SOUL

According to Teutonic mythic tradition, the first man and woman were formed by the gods of consciousness (Woden-Wili-Weh) from trees. Humans are often referred to in the poetic language of the North with arboreal metaphors, all of which points to the essential link between the idea of the tree on the cosmic scale (Yggdrasill) and on the individual human scale. The multidimensional pattern of existence found in the Yggdrasill is also present in the essence of the human being.

Within the Teutonic tradition, the human being is thought to be made up of a complex of factors, all coming together in a certain place and time to give shape to a unique manifestation. Some of these factors may, however, preexist the particular manifestation, or may indeed live on after the present manifestation has dissolved. By the same token, the truth about the

human being is something much more
than what can readily be seen. The ancient
Teutons had dozens of terms for various
aspects of the human body and soul, each
used with a technical accuracy that might
put even a modern psychologist to shame.
Speakers of languages have many terms
for the fine distinctions between things
that they know well. This is why the
Eskimos may have 15 words for "white"—
because they have been sensitized to that
with which they are very familiar.

The individual human being is,
according to Teutonic tradition, really a
body-soul, or psychosomatic complex. The
body is one aspect of this, as are the mind,
the memory (personal as well as collec-
tive), the heart, the will, and certain magickal functions that individuals may or
may not have acquired, or of which some
individuals may have more than one. The
acquisition or the strengthening of these
magickal bodies is one of the main tasks of
Teutonic magick and other spiritual work.
All exercise of the will and consciousness
increases this power.

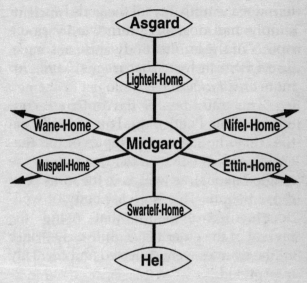

Figure 1: Yggdrasill

ASPECTS OF TEUTONIC MAGIC

The Troth

Teutonic magick is firmly rooted in the essence of the Teutonic religion. This religion is variously known as Odinism (due to the fact that Odin is the chief of the Teutonic gods), as *Ásatrú* , which is an Old Norse term for the troth (*trú*) of the gods (*Æsir*), or simply and most straightforwardly as the troth. The term "troth" is just a simple, direct English word that means "faith," or more exactly, *loyalty*.

The traditions of the troth are contained in the Poetic Edda, the Prose Edda, the Icelandic sagas, other epics of the Teutonic peoples (such as the Beowulf of the Anglo-Saxons), as well as in the folklore of those people. This is a vast body of well-documented evidence that made the revival of the elder ways quite easy—once all the sources were collected and correctly interpreted.

Historically, the fate of the troth was, of course, closely tied to the fate of other aspects of Teutonic spirituality. Whereas the religious aspects tended to find their way into the literary and folkloristic expressions of the Teutons, the more specifically magickal aspects became concealed within, and behind, the new imported magickal forms from the South and East (Rome, Greece, Egypt, and the Middle East). This process of concealment and cultural submersion, along with confusion, went on until fairly recent times when, beginning with the Romantic movement in Europe, people began to look at their own national traditions in an objective but sympathetic way.

Although the history of the revival of the troth can be traced back to the time of its official demise at the hands of medieval evangelists and corrupt monarchs, for our purposes here it is only necessary to outline its most recent phase. At the close of the 1960s, there was a worldwide upsurge in interest in the Teutonic religious traditions. In Germany old societies were renewed; in America and England, new ones were formed. In England, the Odinic Rite was founded, which continues to be the chief exponent of the Teutonic troth in the British Isles today. In this country, there was the Ásatrú Free Assembly, which was decentralized and disbanded in the mid-1980s. This was not due to a lack of interest, but rather to an overabundance of chaotic influences. As a traditional synthesis of the multiformed spirituality of the Teutonic peoples, there has arisen in this country an organization known as the Ring of Troth. The Ring of Troth is a combination of a strictly and traditionally trained priesthood and a loose confederation of local groups called Kindreds.

It is considered the birthright of everyone who feels drawn to the Teutonic troth by their ethnic or spiritual heritage to practice that troth freely and rightly. The troth was the established religion of our ancestors, and most true folk want to make it so again.

One of the mainstays of the troth is the idea that there is a folk-soul. That is, that there is something most would call spiritual that is inherited along genetic lines within a folk-group. Some call this "metagenetics." Ultimately, metagenetics is simply the idea that there is something of a spiritual path encoded in the genetic material of any people. This spiritual path will by its very nature be the path of least resistance to spiritual development of any person belonging to that group.

The Gods and Goddesses

The practitioner of Teutonic spiritual traditions and magick has access to a great wealth of divine magickal archetypes. These gods and goddesses can be approached by the magician in many ways—first, through absorbing the lore and myths of the Teutonic folk, and then through vision quests, magickal invocations and evocations.

From a magickal point of view the chief god and goddess on the Teutonic paths are Woden (known as ódhinn in Old Norse), and Freya (or Freyja). Both are powerful magickal archetypes to be explored by both male and female magicians on the Teutonic paths. These are the models of consciousness that most magicians will seek to emulate in their personal magickal developments.

There is a whole pantheon of magickal archetypes with whom the vitki can deal. The higher divinities are divided into two kinds, the Æsir and the Vanir. The Aesir are the gods and goddesses of social order and consciousness, while the Vanir are the divinities of nature and well-being.

The magickal divinities, Woden and Freya, cross over these boundaries at will.

Woden may be considered the chief god of the vitkis. He is the god of the rune-masters, who attempt to emulate his archetypal pattern in their lives. Woden is a god who sacrifices (gives) "himself to himself" in an act of magickal initiation in order to gain the runes—the knowledge of self and cosmos and the power to act within these realms to effect changes at will.

Among the Æsir—besides Woden, the god of magic, poetry, ecstasy, and divine synthesis of consciousness—there is Tiw, the god of justice and rational thought, and Thunar (Thorr), the god of steadfast loyalty and troth—staunch defender of gods and humanity. Frigga is also an important goddess among the Æsir who influences the maintaining of social order within domestic existence.

Among the Vanir—besides Freya, the goddess of magick and eroticism—there is Freya's twin brother Frey. The names Frey and Freya literally mean "the Lord and the Lady." The form of religion and magick practiced under their auspices in ancient

Anglo-Saxon England was first called by the Old English or Anglo-Saxon word wicca (pronounced "witcha"). Another important Vanic god is Njorth, the father of Freya and Frey, who is the lord of material well-being and plenty.

Actually there are many more gods and goddesses to be explored by the worker of Teutonic magick, but these are the key deities who can open the way to the divine realms.

The chief way in which the elder path of the troth is practiced and the gods and goddesses are honored is through the ritual observation of a sacred cycle of the year. Someone can be said to be "true," that is, loyal to the elder troth if he or she simply observes these times of the year. Things can get much more complicated, of course, but this is the simple essence of the folk-way.

Winter Night (around October 15) is the Norse New Year, which comes at the close of the old harvesting time. The forces of nature are finished expending themselves. This is the beginning of the most important religious phase of the year—the time of midwinter.

Yule (from about December 20 to December 31) is a whole period of time—the old Yuletide, also remembered as the "12 days of Christmas." In this time the whole of the year is magickally contained, and out of it the year is regenerated. The Yuletide begins on Mother Night and ends on Yule itself, 12 nights from the Mother Night.

Disting (around February 14) heralds the beginning of the return of the vital forces that had turned inward at the time of Winter Night, and it is the time when many local assemblies are held.

Easter (Vernal Equinox) is the full manifestation of the return of the vital powers of nature. The name of this celebration was always Teutonic. Eostre is the goddess of the spring and of the dawn. It is simply a name that the Christians could not obliterate.

Walburga/May Day (the nights of April 30 and May 1) is a twofold affair. The night of April 30 is traditionally the "witches" night in central Europe. It is a time when the mysterious night-side of life is strongly manifest. On the other hand,

May Day is quite the opposite, being a bright and sunlit celebration of the day-side of life—of play and of work. May-poles may be erected on this day or Midsummer Day, or both.

Midsummer (North Solstice) is the celebration of the final victory of the Sun in the cycle of the year and of the full mani-festation of the vital forces of nature which were given birth during the Yuletide.

Thing-tide (around August 23) is the time of the great regional or national gath-erings where the social aspects of the troth are given expression. This is the time when legislative and business matters of all kinds are attended to, and when there is a great celebration of the social and organi-zational aspects of the troth.

Harvest/Winter Finding (Autumnal Equinox) begins the culmination of the natural cycle of things that comes into being and passes away toward new begin-nings. The end of this period is celebrated on the Winter Night, bringing the cycle to a close.

It would be a mistake to see this cycle as one simply having to do with the cycles of nature, in the narrower sense of the word; in fact, the mysteries of anything cyclical are contained in this pattern.

The Rituals

The main kind of ritual usually performed during any of these festivals is the blessing. This is a word derived from the Old English bletsian, which meant to perform sacrifice, or more literally, to besprinkle with blood. Only later was it Christianized, like so much else in the religious terminology of the ancient troth. The Old Norse term for this is blót, and it is often used to refer to this kind of rite as well.

The equipment basic to the practice of the troth-blessings consists of an altar (harrow), which can be of stone or wood, a drinking vessel (preferably a drinking horn), a bowl, and a sprig of evergreen. The rites are usually performed outdoors.

The basic blessing formula, which can be adapted to any sacred purpose and can be done to honor or worship any god or goddess, is as follows:

1. *Hallowing*, which sets the ritual time/space apart from the ordinary. This is done most simply by tracing the sign of the hammer in the four cardinal points.
2. *Reading*, which places the rite in a mythic context: mythic poems or epics are read or recited.
3. *Rede*, which links the mythic pattern to the purpose of the ritual at hand. This is a simple or elaborate statement of the main purposes of the rite.
4. *Call*, which invokes the deities or classes of beings to be honored in the rite.
5. *Loading*, which charges the sacred drink with godly power. This is done by pouring the drink—mead (honey wine), ale, beer, or fruit juices—into the drinking vessel and visualizing the collected powers entering into the liquid.
6. *Drinking*, which is the consuming of the charged liquid and internal circulation of its power. This is done by drinking from the horn by all present. The horn is never drained—something is always left, which is poured into the blessing bowl on the altar.

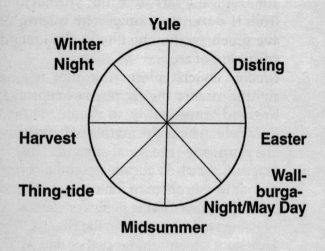

Figure 2: The Holy Calendar

7. *Blessing*, which is the sprinkling of the altar with the sacred liquid. This is done from the sacrificial bowl with a sprig of evergreen, by dipping it in the liquid and sprinkling it around the altar.
8. *Giving*, which is the returning of the rightful part of the gathered power back to the divinity *and/or* to nature. This is done by pouring the contents of the blessing bowl onto the bare earth.
9. *Leaving*, which is the declaration of the end of the work and of the return to the everyday space/time.

This kind of rite can be performed at all of the important times of the year, in honor of all of the gods and goddesses. For a complete system of the religion of the troth, see Edred Thorsson's *A Book of Troth* and Edward Sitch's *Rites of Odin*.

Runes and Magical Signs

The word rune basically and originally means "secret" or "mystery." The runes are really a system of these cosmic mysteries as encoded within the Teutonic mystery school (the ancient rune guild) over 2,000 years ago

These mysteries were encoded in a system of 24 signs, usually now referred to as "runes,"or "runestaves." This original system was modified in later times. It was expanded to 33 runestaves among the Anglo-Saxons, and reduced to 16 signs among the Scandinavians during the so-called Viking Age (from about 800 c.e.).

Each of these systems—as well as the modern German or occult Armanic tradition of Guido von List, Friedrich Marby, Siegfried Kummer, and others—are legitimate esoteric paths. But all of them ultimately stem from the original tradition of the 24 runes of the elder "futhark." The whole system is called futhark because these are the sound values of the first six "letters" of this "alphabet" (see the table below).

The runic system is really a magickal map of the cosmos and of human consciousness. It is a system of magickal learning and a language for the expression of what has been learned. The runic tradition is one that is extremely well documented and chronicled in the annals of the ancient Icelandic sagas and Eddas, as well as in thousands of actual runic inscriptions left behind by the rune-masters of old. One of the most unfortunate aspects of recent runic history is the degree to which the true tradition has been corrupted by the unwise and ignorant scribblings of would-be runemasters. What many have done, is in effect, is to redraw the cosmic map in a way that can lead the seeker astray.

The essence of the runic system can be summed up in the following table:

No.	Shape	Name	Sound	Meaning of Name
1	ᚠ	*fehu*	f	livestock/wealth
2	ᚢ	*uruz*	u	urochs (bison)
3	ᚦ	*thurisaz*	th	giant (thurs)
4	ᚨ	*ansuz*	a	god (Woden)
5	ᚱ	*raidho*	r	a ride (chariot)
6	ᚲ	*kenaz*	k	torch
7	ᚷ	*gebo*	g	gift (sacrifice/hospitality)
8	ᚹ	*wunjo*	w	joy
9	ᚺ	*hagalaz*	h	hail (-stone)
10	ᚾ	*nauthiz*	n	need (distress)
11	ᛁ	*isa*	i	ice
12	ᛃ	*jera*	j	(good-) year, harvest
13	ᛇ	*eihwaz*	ei	yew (World-Tree)

No.	Shape	Name	Sound	Meaning of Name
14	ᛈ	*perthro*	p	lot-cup
15	ᛦ	*elhaz*	-z	elk
16	ᛋ	*sowilo*	s	sun
17	ᛏ	*teiwaz*	t	the god Tiw (Tyr)
18	ᛒ	*berkano*	b	birch (-goddess)
19	ᛖ	*ehwaz*	e	horse
20	ᛗ	*mannaz*	m	human being
21	ᛚ	*laguz*	l	water
22	ᛜ	*ingwaz*	ng	the Earth-god (Ing)
23	ᛞ	*dagaz*	d	day
24	ᛟ	*othila*	o	ancestral property

The whole system of the runes is divided into three *ættir*, or "eights," also known as "families," so that the whole appears like the illustration on page 16.

The whole of the essential runic tradition is in these basic combinations of numbers, shapes, names (and their meanings and esoteric interpretations), and the arrangement in "eights." Any magickal teaching about the runes that does not follow this seed-form is based on nontraditional material and should be viewed with skepticism. Other systems are actually the *personal* concoctions of their creators, while the authentic tradition is *trans*-personal and not the creation of any individual. If it is transpersonal and objective magickal reality that is sought by the vitki, then it only follows that this can best be found in the ancient and authentic tradition.

Runic Ritual

The runes can be used for magickal purposes as a way of actually communicating with other realities. This process can be quite complex and sophisticated in ways very similar to the Hebrew Kabbala. But for basic magickal and divinatory purposes the practice of runic magick can begin quite simply, once the vitki is prepared in the traditions.

As far as ritual is concerned, the simplest form is that of rune-carving itself. The vitki first carves the runes, singing their names as each is carved, and then reddens them with red dye, paint, or blood. Runes are usually carved into wood, but the set of rune cards by Donald Tyson is quite suitable as well.

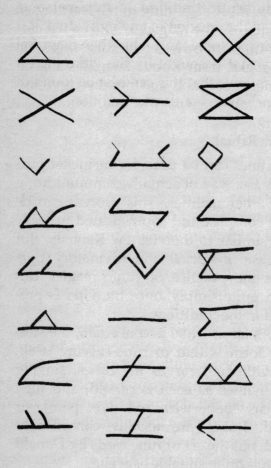

Figure 3: The Runic aettir

An ideal beginning in the learning of the skills of rune magick would be the creation of your own set of runestaves, or rune-sticks, from wood. Take 24 sticks or flat pieces of wood and ritually carve the runes of the futhark into them. This should give the prospective vitki a good sense of the way to work magickally with the runes, and you will have a nice set of runestaves for divinatory purposes as well.

Besides the runestaves there is also the magickal tradition of magickal signs, called galdrastafir in Old Norse, which are used in ways very much akin to the ways in which the runestaves are used. The runes and these magickal signs are both rather like "languages" with which vitkis are able to communicate their wills to the universe, bringing it into accord and harmony with the will of the magician. This is, after all, the essence of magick.

The magickal signs of the ancients can still be used to effect the will of the modern vitki. The most widely known kind of these signs is the ægishjalmr, or "helm of awe." This sign may have as few as four "arms," but it may have many more, and many more sub-branches besides. The most widely known form of the ægishjálmr, looks like the diagram illustrated below:

Figure 4: The Ægishjal mr

Although these signs may be collected and learned by vitkis in order to expand their magickal repertoire, the advanced vitki is also free to construct original *galdrastafir* for special personal aims.

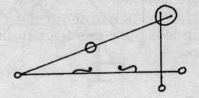

Figure 5: The Draumstafur

The Draumstafur (Dream-Stave): Carve this sign on a piece of fir wood and sleep with it under your pillow or mattress. You will dream whatever you want.

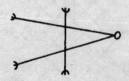

Figure 6: The Dúnfaxi

The Dúnfaxi (Eider-Down—Mane): If you want to win in a law case, carve this sign on a piece of oak wood, and carry it with you to court.

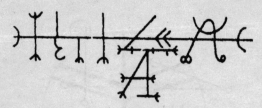

Figure 7: Lukkustafir

Lukkustafir (Luck-Staves): Carve these signs on any kind of wood, or draw them on parchment. Carry them with you always and you will have good luck. These are especially good for travelling.

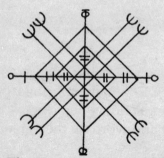

Figure 8: Umbótarstafur

Umbótarstafur (Mending-Stave): Inscribe this sign in red ink on new parchment. It will alleviate any troubles and improve life and provide peace of mind. It is an excellent protective device.

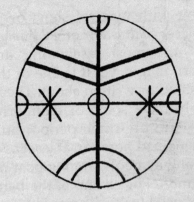

Figure 9: Rótakross

Rótakross (Rota-Cross): This sign, along with many other similar ones, is connected to the SATOR-Square. It brings good fortune and protection when it is inscribed on parchment and worn on the person.

The Magic of Icelandic Galdor-Staves

Working with magical signs or galdor-staves (Ice. *galdrastafir* or *galdramyndir*) is one of the most fascinating areas of Northern magic, yet it is one of the least understood or written about. These signs probably have some of their origins in the obscure pre-runic period, but some have remained popular, at least as curiosity-raising symbols, among post-modern rock bands. For example, the band Psychik TV used Icelandic magical signs on a couple of their albums.

Galdor-staves, as the name suggests, often have something to do with runes. The link with the runes comes in two forms. First, the galdor-staves are sometimes made up of complex runic combinations (bind-runes). These are then perhaps further stylized for magical reasons, or just to make them look more beautiful. Second, the actual magical technique of working with these magical signs is very similar to that of working with runes. With runes the magician carves, colors, and sings the right rune songs, while with galdor-staves the magician simply writes or draws the sign, then speaks or sings an incantation or "prayer" formula to charge the sign.

The major historical period of activity for galdor-stave magicians in Iceland was in the Middle Ages and during the Reformation (1000-1750). Although there are examples of such magic from all over the Scandinavian countries, Iceland seems to have preserved or developed the tradition most vigorously.

Over time there seems to have been an "evolution" of this magical practice from strictly runic techniques to that of the galdor-staves. On the other hand, perhaps the galdor-stave tradition is just as old (if not older) than that of the runes and it is just that the signs simply continued being used after formal rune magic had gone into decline.

Most of what we know of the use of galdor-staves comes from a number of manuscripts called, in Icelandic, *galdrabækur* (books of magic). Only one of these survives completely intact—the so-called *Galdrabók*. This book, along with other similar historical documents, has been translated in *The Galdrabók* (Weiser,

1989). The rest of the material survives in fragments and collections made by humanistic antiquarians or philologists in the 1600s and after.

There were two famous and legendary magical manuscripts in Iceland. One was called Gráskinni (Gray-Leather). It consisted of two parts, the first in the regular Roman alphabet and the other in some kind of runic code (Ice. villurúnir, erring runes). Another, and yet more powerful book, was called Raudhskinni (Red-Leather). It is said to have been compiled by Bishop Gottskálk. He was bishop at Holar in Iceland from 1497 to 1520. Raudhskinni is supposed to have been written in golden runes on red parchment (hence the name of the manuscript). The bishop is said to have been buried with the book. Since he had not taught all of its "heathen" secrets to his living students, the book remains a legendary "lost key" to magical power.

Bishop Gottskálk is only one of the famous magicians of Icelandic lore. In the time just after the "conversion" of Iceland to Christianity, there lived the godhi (priest-chieftain) Sæmundur the Wise (1056-1133). He and his sister Holla were said to be "good" magicians, even though they derived their magical power from "heathen lore."

The Icelanders widely regarded magic as being something derived chiefly from their pagan past. In the spells in these books, we can see the old Gods and Goddesses being called upon more then half a millennium after their official demise. In fact, it is fair to say the old Gods never died in Iceland.

Besides the magicians of good reputation, there were others with darker images. Bishop Gottskálk was one of these. In later times, the mysterious figure of Galdra-Loptur (who died in 1722) tried to raise the long dead Bishop Gottskálk from his grave in order to gain possession of the long hidden secrets contained in Raudhskinni. But Gottskálk was able to keep his secrets and Galdra-Loptur was left spiritually and mentally shattered by the experience.

Typically these books, or grimoires, were rather like recipe books. They would show the sign or stave and perhaps give the incantation or other prayer formulas to be used in conjunction with the sign. But they never went into the years of preparation the magician would have to go through to make the magic really work.

Perhaps an old offshoot of the Teutonic magick practices, hex signs have been used as meaningful ornamentation throughout the United States. The so-called Pennsylvania Dutch (perhaps more properly, "German," as they migrated for the most part from southwestern Germany) have been avid practitioners of what they call *hexerei* or *brauche*.

In at least one branch of this practice, it is held that the *Hexenmeister* should carefully construct a *hexezeichen* (hex-sign) for the specific purpose of the magickal working, and speak or chant an incantation over it to load it with individual willpower.

Figure 11: The Distelfink

This sign brings good fortune into the general environment. The Distelfink rules over the heart. Good fortune reigns in the heart, and the tulip has faith and loyalty in love. The Distelfink should be painted with a yellow (divine love) body, red (emotional) head and wings along with a green (good fortune) tail. Both the heart and tulips should be red on the outside with yellow on the inside. The sign should be displayed in the living area of the house.

The magical power sign is projected out from a dynamic and balanced threefold spiritual core (blue and white) through an eightfold star (permanent and manifested order) in the inner world. The inner world is also filled with faith and trust (tulips). The star is violet (power) and blue (truth) and the tulips are red (vitality). This combined dynamic core and ordered inner world of power and truth tempered by trust are projected into the objective world through red (action) chevrons. This sign should be kept private or displayed in your work area.

Figure 12: Magical Power

A typical hex-sign for love and loyalty to ensure a happy marriage would be:

Figure 13: The Marriage Hex-Sign

These hex-signs and the magick surrounding their tradition serve as another fertile field of exploration for the Teutonic magician.

Seidhr
(Shamanism)

Besides the practice of galster (or *galdr*) in the Teutonic tradition, there is also the kind of magick known in Old Norse as *seidhr*. In seidhr the vitki seeks experience outside him/herself, seeks to submerge his/her mind and consciousness into an otherworldly state—to travel to other dimensions of reality in order to do magickal work and to learn things of the world and of him/herself.

In many ways the practice of seidhr is virtually identical to that which is often called shamanism today. Through the practice of seidhr the vitki can shape-shift and gain visions from the realms beyond. Quite often the practice of seidhr may also involve sexual activity, very much akin to the practices of tantrism or sex magick.

In the ancient Teutonic traditions it is related how Woden (Ódhinn) was taught the mysteries of seidhr by the Vanic goddess Freya. It is also likely that Woden shared his knowledge of galdr with Freya. If this is considered, a picture of balance emerges.

To work seidhr the vitki must first achieve an altered state of consciousness. Traditionally this was done with a variety or combination of techniques, including drugs, sleep deprivation, fasting, sensory overload, and even physical tortures, which might be combined with ritual chanting, dancing, and perhaps the playing of some rhythmic instrument. There is no evidence that a drum was a regular part of the Teutonic form of shamanism, but that is no compelling reason why one could not be experimented with today. Once in this shamanic trance state, the vitki contemplates some mythic landscape, such as that of the realms of Yggdrasill. In the roots and branches of the World-Tree, the vitki can search for his or her otherworldly mate, magickal or protective spirit (*fetch*), or animal spirit (*fetch-animal*). In ancient times it is said that the most powerful seidhrmen and women could actually send out a part of their souls to take on the shape of a mighty beast to fight their battles, while their natural bodies lay as if they were dead.

The simplest working form of seidhr would be the practice of sitting at a crossroad or on a hilltop to hold a vigil for seeking a vision of your fetch-animal or fetch-wife or man. To do this, simply sit at one of the appropriate locations during the nighttime hours. You could chant or sing the names of the runes and/or read poetic stanzas from the *Poetic Edda*. But what is really most authentic is probably the chanting of lines in the "tongue of the gods," which is a completely non-natural, purely emotional language. This is usually made up of what might seem to be random and often repetitive combinations of consonants and vowels. Combinations such as "fa-la-la-la-la" and "fi-fei-fo-fum" may have their origins in such practices. The main point would be to find a personal combination of sounds and notes that work for you individually. The important thing is to get into the state of mind so seidhr can be performed.

Once this state is reached, the vitki waits for some indication, by physical vision or through magickal imagination, of what the fetch-animal is. Most will sink into a light trance state, which will enhance their powers of visualization. In this state the fetch-animal or fetch-wife or man could give the vitki further instructions on what to do and what paths to follow.

The Teutonic Role in the Western Tradtion

The Germanic or Teutonic peoples have their own special and unique forms of magickal practice, such as rune-galster or seither, but the Teutonic influence on the development of what we generally call the Western Occult, or Magickal Tradition has been very great indeed, especially in the last 600 years.

From the time of the Renaissance it was especially the Teutonic or Germanic magicians and alchemists who lent a new spirit of scientific method and systematic thoroughness to the pursuit of magick. This magic spirit was to become the cornerstone of the later occult revival in the late 19th century with such lodges as the Golden Dawn.

Among the names of Teutonic magicians most responsible for the establishment of the tradition of occult science, the most prominent are Theophrastus Bombastus von Hohenheim—Paracelsus, and Cornelius von Nettesheim—Agrippa. It has chiefly been from the work of these men that the techniques of high magick in the Western Tradition have been derived. Their work represents a synthesis of the inherited Hermetic tradition and the indigenous European, or Teutonic tradition. The latter tradition has been clearer in the ways in which they worked and the aims of their workings, rather than in the symbolism which they used.

A major school of esoteric thought also arose in Germany during the period of the Northern Renaissance known as the Rosicrucianism. This system of thought influenced esoteric philosophy from the early 1600s onward. It really represents a grand synthesis of the medieval mystomagical arts (including magick and alchemy) and thrusts them into the Age of Enlightenment—where they are to affect the worlds of science and statecraft.

The Faustian Tradition

One of the most famous figures of Teutonic magickal history is Dr. Faustus. He is highly significant to the understanding of the "darker" side of the Teutonic tradition. Although there seems to have been a historical personage by the name Johann Faust, who gained a reputation for having sold his soul to a demon for magickal powers, it is more in the realm of literature, folklore and magickal mythology that the Faustian archetype takes on its chief importance for the history of Teutonic magick.

Originally the story of Faust was told and retold to warn would-be sorcerers away from dealings with the devil. However, the practical occult literature of the time, the grimoires, shows that the archetype of Faust was indeed being used as a model for magicians attempting to follow the Faustian path. As European civilization began to throw off the burden laid on it by the evangelists, a new attitude toward the Faustian path emerged. This feeling is best exemplified in the work of J. W. von Goethe, whose Faust really represents the first Faustian tale by a Faustian man.

Dr. Faustus
Etching by Rembrandt.

**Figure 14: Dr. Faustus,
an etching by Rembrandt**

The essence of the Faustian path is the will of the magician to give (or "sell") a part of him/herself to another part—to risk its ultimate loss in exchange for *knowledge* and *power*. The clear relationship between this and the Odian path is obvious. What is also obvious, however, is the typical Teutonic willingness to deal in the realms of "darkness" in order to emerge into a wholly new kind of light like none other experienced before.

Saturnian Magick

In the early part of this century, there arose in Germany a magickal order that some say was a revival or continuation of a much older order dedicated to the principles embodied in the demiurge Saturn. This is the Fraternitas Saturni, founded on Thelemic lines in the late 1920s by Gregor A. Gregorius. This order remains the most important exponent of the Western Magickal Tradition in Germany. The work of the order represents a synthesis of Germanic traditions along with the magickal principles of Freemasonry, Templarism,

Rosicrucianism, sexual magick, Kabbalism, Thelemism, and Astrosophy, or the magick of the planets and stars.

The Brotherhood of Saturn plays much the same role in Germany as the Golden Dawn does in Anglo-American occultism. The order was, and is, a rich storehouse of magickal teachings, which are only now becoming available in the English-speaking world. Some of these teachings carry a dark aspect, but it is in the darkness where the light of humanity shines the brightest and is most free and manifest as an independent magickal agent in the universe. This free interplay of the darkness and the light is a strong feature of practically all forms of the Teutonic tradition. Perhaps it stems back to the original cosmic model of the Teutons—fire and ice—but for whatever reason, the Teutonic magician seems to love the interplay of darkness and light and to take delight in the state of flux created between them.

The Dark Side

There can be no doubt that the Teutonic spirit is one that loves the night as well as

the Sun light. But this darkness is not evil in the sense most would understand it today. It is merely the night-side of reality, the night-side of the soul and of nature. This is all a legitimate part of exploration of the Teutonic paths.

In this century, however, we have seen the outbreak of another aspect, which has been interpreted by many as an expression of the Teutonic spirit: Nazism, or National Socialism and its offshoots. This association of Teutonic mysticism and Nazism is not difficult to make, as the Nazis themselves exploited this connection to their own ends. But if you study the original traditions of the Teutons you will find very little to support Hitler's ideas. The members of the Nazi Party were to some extent manipulators of reality through Teutonic imagery (which was very popular in the mass German mind at the time), and to some extent they were themselves products of the Zeitgeist—the spirit of the times—in which these images were so popular. But in reality the Nazi period was not an essential expression of Teutonic spirituality. The ancient Teutons were freedom-loving, individualistic, tribal folk who would have had little in common with the totalitarian, collectivist state conjured up by Hitler and his associates—no matter how it was packaged. Most works purporting to connect Nazism with sinister cosmic plots or Satanic conspiracies are merely the products of their authors' lurid imaginations and fantasies.

There was a true groundswell of Teutonic spirituality in German-speaking Europe during the early part of this century, but it was largely destroyed by the Nazis, not supported by them. Unfortunately, many of the admirers of this form of spirituality do not recognize this fact even today!

THE FUTURE

Teutonic magick at present is much like a sapling of oak. It has been grown from the acorn inherited from days of yore, but it is essentially a new and flexible organism. The Teutonic tradition is every bit as rich and varied as the Hermetic or Kabbalistic.

At this stage in its rebirth, however, there is a great opportunity—and a certain danger inherent in that opportunity—for individuals and groups to effectively contribute to the shape of the final oak tree that this tradition will again eventually become. The danger is that the young tree can be misshapen through ignorant and unwise attempts to alter its natural growth. It has survived one of these attempts, but it remains unknown as to how many more such episodes it could take.

If the Teutonic troth is to fulfill its destiny—its wyrd—with all its magick then it will have to be guided by wise and knowledgeable folk.

STAY IN TOUCH

On the following pages you will find some of the books now available on related subjects. Your book dealer stocks most of these and will stock new titles in the Llewellyn series as they become available. We urge your patronage.

To obtain our full catalog write for our bimonthly news magazine/catalog, *Llewellyn's New Worlds of Mind and Spirit*. A sample copy is free, and it will continue coming to you at no cost as long as you are an active mail customer. Or you may subscribe for just $10.00 in the U.S.A. and Canada ($20.00 overseas, first class mail). Many bookstores also have *New Worlds* available to their customers. Ask for it.

Llewellyn's New Worlds of Mind and Spirit
P.O. Box 64383-799, St. Paul, MN 55164-0383, U.S.A.

TO ORDER BOOKS AND TAPES

If your book dealer does not have the books described, you may order them directly from the publisher by sending full price in U.S. funds, plus $3.00 for postage and handling for orders under $10.00; $4.00 for orders *over* $10.00. There are no postage and handling charges for orders over $50.00. Postage and handling rates are subject to change. We ship UPS whenever possible. Delivery guaranteed. Provide your street address as UPS does not deliver to P.O. Boxes. UPS to Canada requires a $50.00 minimum order. Allow 4-6 weeks for delivery. Orders outside the U.S.A. and Canada: Airmail—add retail price of book; add $5.00 for each non-book item (tapes, etc.); add $1.00 per item for surface mail. Mail orders to:

LLEWELLYN PUBLICATIONS
P.O. BOX 64383-799, St. Paul, MN 55164-0383, U.S.A.

A BOOK OF TROTH
by Edred Thorsson

A Book of Troth presents for the first time the essence of Teutonic neo-paganism between two covers. It is a must for anyone interested in an effective system based on ancient and timeless principles.

One of the most widespread of the ancient pagan revivals is Asatru or Odinism. Its followers seek to rekindle the way of the North, of the ancient Teutonic peoples. Until now, no book has completely expressed the nature and essence of this movement. *A Book of Troth* is that book.

It is the most traditionally based and well-informed general guide to the practice of the elder Germanic folk way. The official document of the organization known simply as the "Ring of Troth," *A Book of Troth* is not a holy book or bible in the usual sense. Rather it outlines a code of behavior and a set of actions, not a doctrine or way of believing.

A person's deeds are considered much more important than the doctrine to which he or she holds. Much of this "true work" is done in one's everyday life, to be sure. But what is most essential is taking part in the four Greatest Blessings of the Year: Winter Nights, Yule, Easter and Midsummer. The "Ring of Troth" promotes a multiplicity of approaches to the gods and goddesses, for the realities of these beings are many and have many levels—all true.

The first section of the book explores the various important themes or teachings of the religion, laying the intellectual groundwork for the practice. The second section is the heart of the book, since the Troth is a way of doing, not of believing. Here the reader learns how to actually practice the various religious observances with complete rituals, the tools needed, timing, and proper arrangement of the sacred space. The third part of the book outlines the curriculum and training program for qualifying as a priest, priestess, or Elder in the Troth.

0-87542-777-4, 5 ¼ x 8, illus., 248 pgs. $9.95

RUNE MIGHT
by Edred Thorsson

Rune Might reveals, for the first time in the English language, the long-hidden secrets of the German rune magicians who practiced their arts in the beginning of this century. Most of their work has been unavailable even in German for several decades.

By studying the contents of *Rune Might* and working with the exercises, the reader will be introduced to a fascinating world of magical personalities and the sometimes sinister dark corners of runic history. Beyond this, the reader will be able to experience the direct power of the runes as experienced by the early German rune magicians.

For those who have recently rediscovered the magic of the runes, this book provides a useful supplement. The magical heritage of the runes will become clearer to those who experience their power through the formulae that gave the first magical impulse to the runic revival.

Rune Might takes the most powerful of the runic techniques developed in that early phase of the runic revival and offers them as a coherent set of exercises. Experience rune yoga, rune dance, runic hand gestures (mudras), rune singing (mantras), group rites with runes, runic healing, runic geomancy, and two of the most powerful runic methods of engaging transpersonal powers—the Ritual of the Ninth Night and the Ritual of the Grail Cup.

The exercises represent bold new methods of drawing magical power into your life—regardless of the magical tradition or system with which you normally work. Rune exercises can be incorporated into any magical curriculum. The runes can be used to focus various qualities of magical force—as absorbed from the Earth, the atmosphere, or the outer reaches of the cosmos—in the personal sphere of the magician. No other system does this in quite the direct and clearly defined ways that rune exercises do.

0-87542-778-2, 5¼ x 8, illus., 192 pgs. $7.95